A Benjamin Blog and his Inquisitive Dog Guide

Spain

Anita Ganeri

heinemann raintree

To contact Capstone Global Library please phone 800-747-4992, or visit our website
www.capstonepub.com

Edited by Helen Cox Cannons
Designed by Philippa Jenkins and Tim Bond
Original illustrations © Capstone Global Library Limited 2015
Original map illustration by Oxford Designers and Illustrators
Ben and Barko Illustrated by Sernur ISIK
Picture research by Svetlana Zhurkin
Production by Helen McCreath
Originated by Capstone Global Library Limited
Printed and bound in China by CTPS

19 18 17 16 15
10 9 8 7 6 5 4 3 2 1

Library of Congress Cataloging-in-Publication Data
Ganeri, Anita, 1961-
  Spain / Anita Ganeri.
    pages cm.—(Country guides, with Benjamin Blog and his inquisitive dog)
  Includes bibliographical references and index.
    ISBN 978-1-4109-7996-4 (hb)—ISBN 978-1-4109-8002-1 (pb)—ISBN 978-1-4109-8013-7 (ebook) 1. Spain—
Juvenile literature. I. Title.

DP17.G25 2015
946—dc23   2014043977

This book has been officially leveled by using the F&P Text Level Gradient™ Leveling System.

Acknowledgments
The author and publisher are grateful to the following for permission to reproduce copyright material:
Alamy: Agencja Fotograficzna Caro, 16; Dreamstime: Arnel Manalang, 7, Lucavanzolini, 12, Luisrsphoto, 27,
29; iStockphoto: OJO_Images, 15; Newscom: Album/Jordi Longas, 8, Alfaqui Fotografia/Cesar Cebolla, 22,
Danita Delimont Photography/Walter Bibikow, 10, EPA/Enrique de la Osa, 23; Shutterstock: bonchan, 21,
Carlos Violda, 11, Darios, 25, Gil C, 28, Iakov Filimonov, 4, 19, JBDesign, 9, KarSol, 13, Kiev.Victor, 14, Marco
Mayer, 20, Marques, cover, 26, Natursports, 18, Philip Bird LRPS CPAGB, 17; SuperStock: age footstock, 24,
National Geographic/Tino Soriano, 6.

Some words are shown in bold, **like this.** You can find
out what they mean by looking in the glossary.

Contents

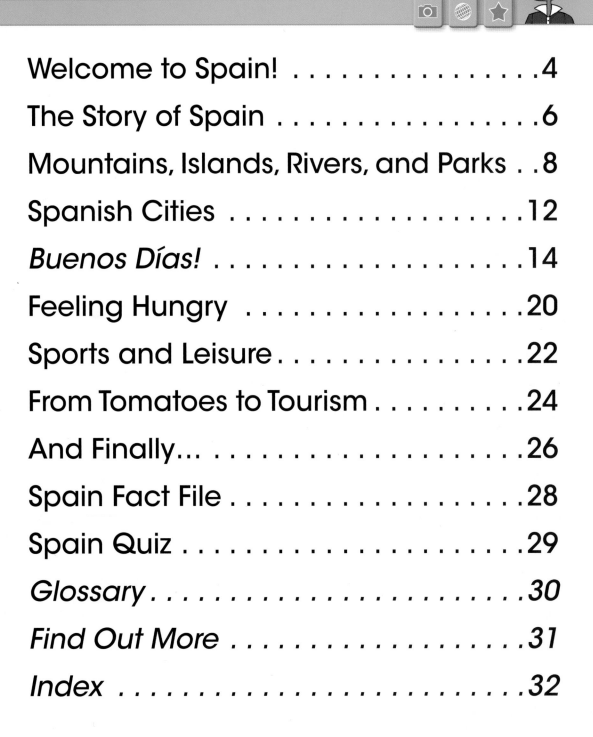

Welcome to Spain!

Hello! My name is Benjamin Blog, and this is Barko Polo, my **inquisitive** dog. (He is named after the ancient explorer **Marco Polo**.) We have just returned from our latest adventure— exploring Spain. We put this book together from some of the blog posts we wrote along the way.

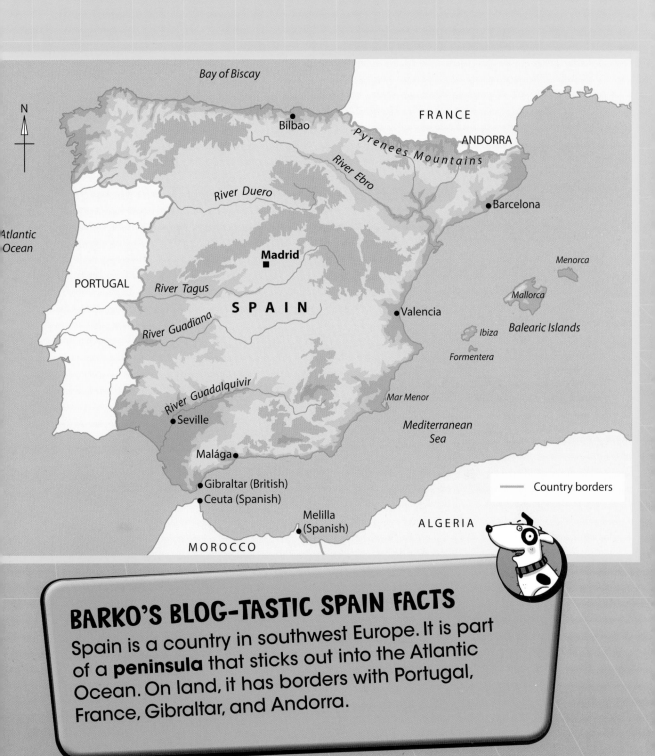

Bay of Biscay

FRANCE

Bilbao

Pyrenees Mountains

ANDORRA

River Ebro

River Duero

Barcelona

Atlantic
Ocean

Menorca

Madrid

Mallorca

PORTUGAL

River Tagus

S P A I N

Valencia

Balearic Islands

River Guadiana

Ibiza

Formentera

River Guadalquivir

Mar Menor

Seville

Mediterranean
Sea

Malága

Gibraltar (British)

Ceuta (Spanish)

Country borders

Melilla
(Spanish)

ALGERIA

MOROCCO

N

BARKO'S BLOG-TASTIC SPAIN FACTS

Spain is a country in southwest Europe. It is part of a **peninsula** that sticks out into the Atlantic Ocean. On land, it has borders with Portugal, France, Gibraltar, and Andorra.

The Story of Spain

Posted by: Ben Blog | March 6 at 10:03 a.m.

We are here at the Altamira Cave in northern Spain, on the first stop of our tour. I wanted to see the famous cave paintings that were made by **prehistoric** people thousands of years ago. You can't go inside the original cave, but a **replica** has been built next door. Look at that **bison**!

BARKO'S BLOG-TASTIC SPAIN FACTS

In the 15th and 16th centuries, many explorers set out from Spain to find new **trade routes** around the world. One of the most famous was Cristóbal Colón. He is now known as Christopher Columbus.

Mountains, Islands, Rivers, and Parks

Posted by: Ben Blog | April 19 at 2:21 p.m.

Our next stop was the Pyrenees, a mountain range that lies along the border with France. It stretches for about 270 miles (430 kilometers) and is an amazing place to explore. We're off to climb Pico de Aneto, the highest peak in the Pyrenees. See you in around 12 hours!

From the Pyrenees, we headed a short way south to Zaragoza. The city stands on the Ebro, the longest river in Spain. The Ebro flows for 565 miles (910 kilometers), from the mountains in Cantabria into the Mediterranean Sea. I'm standing on the Puente de Piedra bridge across the river.

I am here!

BARKO'S BLOG-TASTIC SPAIN FACTS

Doñana National Park is an area of marshes, streams, and sand dunes in southern Spain. Here, the Guadalquivir River flows into the sea. The national park is home to the very rare Iberian lynx.

Spanish Cities

Posted by: Ben Blog | June 14 at 3:30 p.m.

Today, we headed to Madrid, the capital city of Spain. Barko took this photo of me at the Royal Palace. The royal family of Spain lives here. This is one of the biggest palaces in Europe. It has more than 3,000 rooms! We're about to set off on a tour—I hope we don't get lost.

BARKO'S BLOG-TASTIC SPAIN FACTS

The city of Barcelona is packed with amazing buildings. This is the Sagrada Família. It is a huge church, designed by the **architect** Antoni Gaudí. It has never been finished!

Buenos Días!

Posted by: Ben Blog | July 26 at 12:45 p.m.

Most Spanish people speak Spanish. Spanish is also spoken by millions of people around the world. I've been trying to learn a few words. *Buenos días!* means "Good day," but you can also say *Hola!* ("Hello"). *Por favor* is "please," and *gracias* is "thank you."

BARKO'S BLOG-TASTIC SPAIN FACTS

Family life is very important in Spain. People sometimes move away from their families to find work, but they like to get together in their spare time and help to look after each other.

It is 9:00 a.m., and these Spanish children are starting school. For some children, the school day finishes at 2:00 p.m. In the summer, students have a long break that lasts from June until September. They have shorter breaks at Christmas and Easter.

BARKO'S BLOG-TASTIC SPAIN FACTS

In Andalucía, in southern Spain, "white towns" like this one are dotted across the hills. All of the houses have **whitewashed** walls and get a fresh coat of paint every year.

Many Spanish people are **Roman Catholics**, and there are beautiful churches all around Spain. We've arrived in Santiago de Compostela. People come here from around the world to visit the cathedral. Some of them walk long distances to get here, as a sign of their faith.

BARKO'S BLOG-TASTIC SPAIN FACTS

Every year, in August, a very messy festival takes place in the town of Buñol. It is called La Tomatina. Thousands of people line the streets and throw tomatoes at each other for fun.

Feeling Hungry

Posted by: Ben Blog | November 15 at 1:06 p.m.

For lunch today, we decided to try paella, a famous Spanish dish. It is made of rice mixed with **seafood**, meat, tomatoes, peppers, and saffron. It was so tasty that I had seconds! I'm looking forward to a siesta—a short nap you take after lunch.

BARKO'S BLOG-TASTIC SPAIN FACTS

Savory snacks called tapas are very popular all over Spain. You can dig into *patatas bravas* (spicy potatoes), tortilla (Spanish omelette), chorizo (spicy sausage), olives, or juicy shrimp like these. Yum!

Sports and Leisure

Posted by: Ben Blog | December 29 at 3:12 p.m.

Back in Madrid, we're at the Bernabéu Stadium to watch a soccer match. Real Madrid is playing. It is one of the top Spanish teams. Soccer is the most popular sport in Spain, and the fans here really get behind their team. *Hala*, Madrid! (Go, Madrid!)

BARKO'S BLOG-TASTIC SPAIN FACTS

Pelota is a Spanish ball game played by two teams on a walled court. The players hit the ball with their hands or with wooden bats or baskets. The aim is to put the ball out of the other team's reach.

From Tomatoes to Tourism

Posted by: Ben Blog | February 3 at 2:56 p.m.

We're in Almeria, in southern Spain, visiting a tomato farm. Here, tomatoes, melons, and peppers are grown in plastic greenhouses and sold all over Europe. Spanish farmers also grow crops such as oranges, olives, almonds, and grapes, for making wine.

BARKO'S BLOG-TASTIC SPAIN FACTS

Tourism is very important in Spain and earns lots of money for the country. Millions of vacationers visit Spain each year to enjoy the sunny weather and beautiful beaches.

And Finally...

It's our last day, and we have come to the Alhambra Palace in Granada. It was built in the 13th to 14th centuries by a **Moorish** king. I took this photo in the Court of the Lions. The fountain is held up by 12 white marble lions. Water spurts from the lions' mouths.

The Guggenheim in Bilbao is a spectacular museum. The building is covered in gleaming glass, **titanium**, and **limestone**. Inside, there are exhibitions by famous artists and sculptors.

Spain Fact File

Area: 195,124 square miles
(505,370 square kilometers)

Population: 46,704,314 (2013)

Capital city: Madrid

Other main cities: Barcelona, Valencia, Seville

Languages: Spanish (Castilian), Catalan,
Gallego, Euskera (Basque)

Main religion: Christianity (**Roman Catholic**)

Highest mountain: Pico de Teide
(12,198 feet/3,718 meters)

Longest river: Ebro (565 miles/910 kilometers)

Currency: Euro

Spain Quiz

Find out how much you know about Spain with our quick quiz.

1. Which mountains lie between Spain and France?
a) Alps
b) Pyrenees
c) Rock of Gibraltar

2. Which is the longest river in Spain?
a) Ebro
b) Tagus
c) Guadalquivir

3. How do you say "thank you" in Spanish?
a) *Por favor*
b) *Hola*
c) *Gracias*

4. What are tapas?
a) a type of meal
b) a type of dancing
c) a type of fish

5. What is this?

Answers
1. b
2. a
3. c
4. a
5. Guggenheim, Bilbao

Glossary

active volcano volcano that is still erupting

architect person who designs buildings

bison large, bull-like animal with a huge head, shaggy hair, and a humped back

inquisitive interested in learning about the world

limestone hard rock used as a building material

Marco Polo explorer who lived from about 1254 to 1324. He traveled from Italy to China.

Moorish relating to the Moors, Muslims who ruled parts of Spain during medieval times

peninsula thin strip of land that sticks out into the sea

prehistoric from a time long ago, before things were written down

replica exact copy of something

Roman Catholic Christian who belongs to the Roman Catholic Church

seafood food from the sea, such as shrimp, squid, and lobster

titanium strong, white metallic material

trade route sea journey taken by sailing ships to buy and sell goods in other countries

whitewashed painted with white paint

Find Out More

Books

Guillain, Charlotte. *Spain* (Countries Around the World). Chicago: Heinemann Library, 2012.

Ryan, Sean. *Spain in Our World* (Countries in Our World). Mankato, Minn.: Smart Apple Media, 2011.

Savery, Annabel. *Spain* (Been There!). Mankato, Minn.: Smart Apple Media, 2012.

Web sites

Facthound offers a safe, fun way to find Internet sites related to this book. All of the sites on Facthound have been researched by our staff.

Here's all you do:

Visit www.facthound.com

Type in this code: 9781410979964

Index

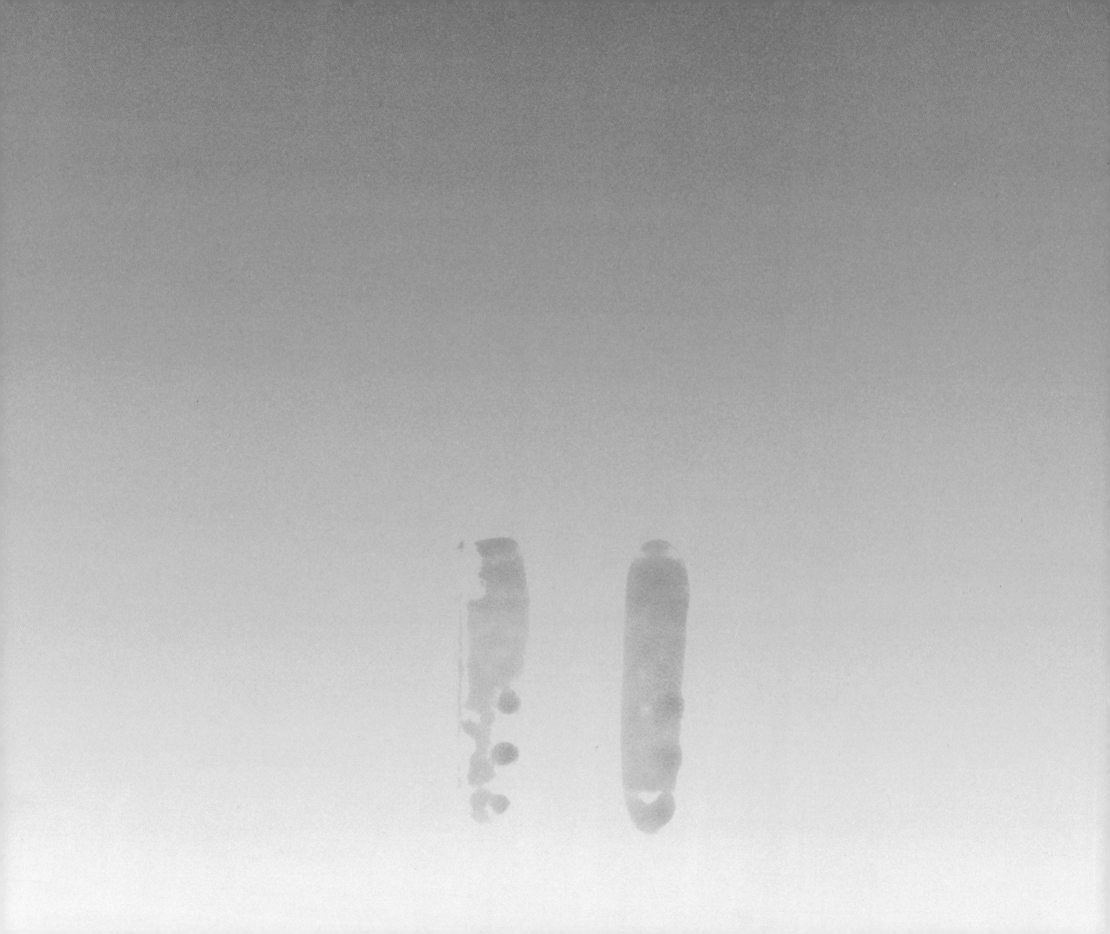

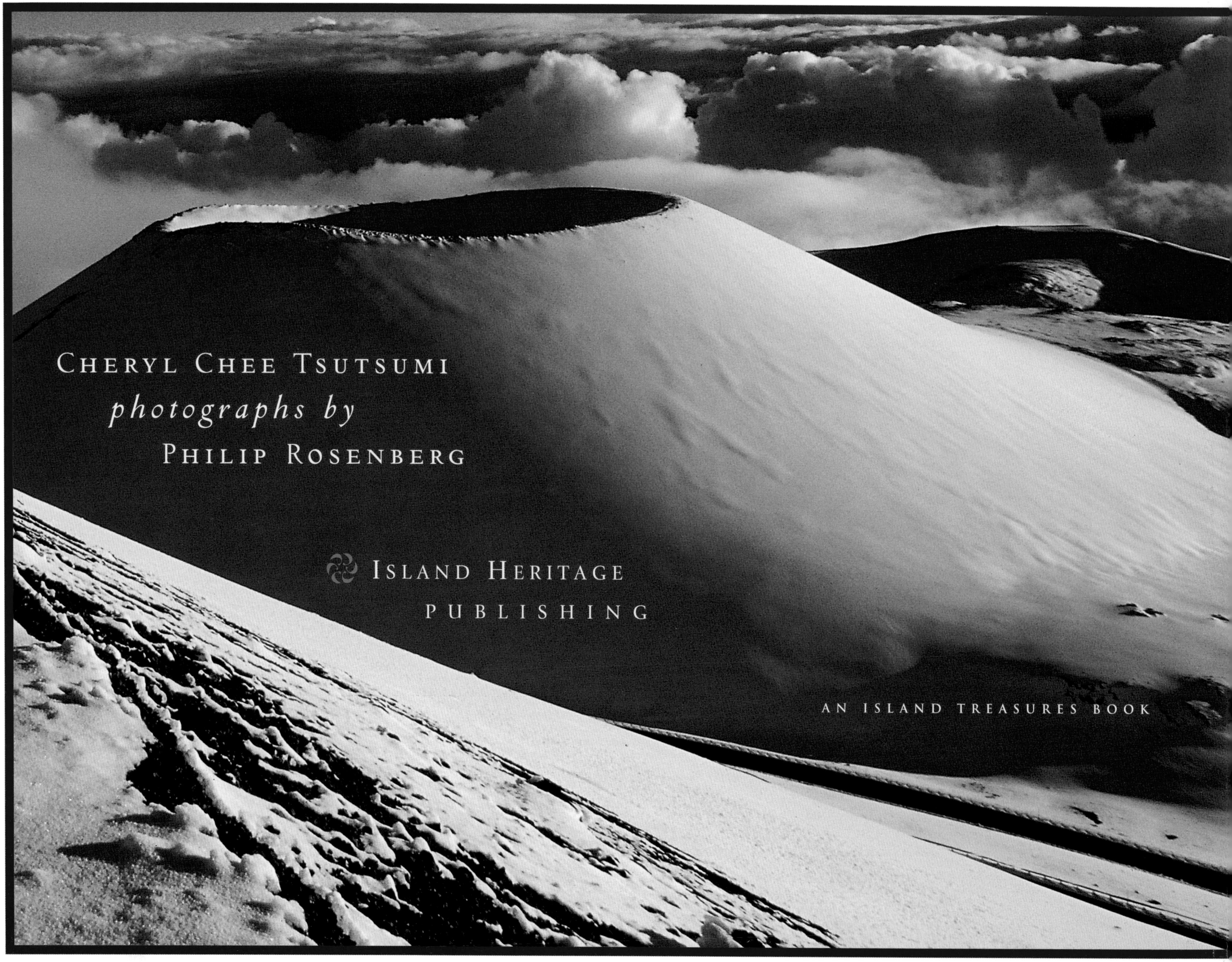

Cheryl Chee Tsutsumi

photographs by

Philip Rosenberg

Island Heritage

PUBLISHING

AN ISLAND TREASURES BOOK

LAND of FIRE & ICE

THE BIG ISLAND

Published and distributed by
ISLAND HERITAGE PUBLISHING

ISBN 0-89610-396-X

Address orders and correspondence to:

 ISLAND HERITAGE
PUBLISHING
99-880 Iwaena Street
Aiea, Hawaii 96701-3202
Fax 808-488-2279
Telephone 808-487-7299
hawaii4u@islandheritage.com

Printed in Hong Kong
First Edition, First Printing, 2000

EDITED BY VIRGINIA WAGEMAN
DESIGNED BY JIM WAGEMAN

*S*unset ignites the sky over 'Anaeho'omalu Bay on the Kohala Coast.

Contents

Welcome

TO THE BIG ISLAND

Sultry and demure, lush and austere, perky and subdued—the island of Hawai'i, appropriately called the Big Island, presents an amazing range of moods and faces. It's as though the Almighty Creator wasn't quite sure what to do with its 4,038 square miles, so he blessed it with a bit of everything.

Within an hour or so you can go from sweltering desert to cool rain forest, from palm-fringed beach to snow-capped peak. In fact, geographically speaking, the Big Island is the most diverse in the Hawaiian chain, boasting eleven of the thirteen official climates known throughout the world (only arctic and extreme desert conditions aren't found here).

The seven other major Hawaiian islands can fit within its borders with plenty of room to spare, but "big" only begins to describe its many wonders. Think superlatives. Barely eight hundred thousand years old, the Big Island is the youngest island in the Hawaiian archipelago. It claims the southernmost point (Ka Lae) and the wettest city (Hilo) in the United States. America's only commercially grown chocolate is produced in Kea'au, on the east side of the island, and the country's finest commercially grown coffee (priced at about $35 per precious pound) thrives in Kona, on the west side.

The early Hawaiians had no written language, so the hula was used to record genealogy, history, and important events in their lives. This graceful dancer (left) performs at a hula festival in Ka'ū.

Sun worshippers stake out their spot on the sands of 200-foot-wide Hāpuna Beach, the widest white sand beach on the Big Island.

Measuring sixty miles long and thirty miles wide, and containing ten thousand cubic miles of solid rock, Mauna Loa is the largest mountain in the world. More than 90 percent of the stars visible from Earth can be seen from atop nearby Mauna Kea, where the W. M. Keck Observatory houses the world's largest optical/infrared telescopes.

Hawaiian history is peppered with tales about Kamehameha I, the first in a long, proud line of monarchs who ruled Hawai'i for nearly a century. This great warrior king, who is credited with unifying all the islands under one rule, was born in the North Kohala district around 1758. His parents were Keōuakupuapāikalaninui, the chief of the area, and Keku'iapoiwa, a chiefess who hailed from Kona.

Before Kamehameha was born, a *kahuna* (priest) supposedly predicted that the son of Keōuakupuapāikalaninui and Keku'iapoiwa would grow up to be a "conqueror of chiefs." Hearing this prophecy, worried rulers in the Kohala region planned to kidnap the couple's child if it was a boy and murder him. Keōua-kupuapāikalaninui and Keku'iapoiwa learned of the plot, so when it was time for her to give birth, she stole away to the royal birthing stones near Mo'okini Heiau and delivered her baby in secrecy.

Fearing for the safety of her son, Keku'iapoiwa gave him to a trusted servant with the instructions that he be cared for surreptitiously. The servant carried Kamehameha to remote Waipi'o Valley, where he was raised for the first years of his life virtually in solitude. Fittingly, Kamehameha means "the lonely one."

*M*embers of the Aloha Festivals' royal court participate in a ceremony at Halema'uma'u Crater, Volcano.

When he was five, Kamehameha returned to his parents. As he matured, he proved his prowess as a soldier, statesman, and athlete, excelling in sports like surfing, hand wrestling, and spear throwing. He stood a regal six-and-a-half feet tall, had a muscular build, and was renowned for his strength.

Before Hawai'i was unified, rival chiefs constantly waged war to gain power and land. Kamehameha led many destructive raids on villages and fishing expeditions throughout the islands. During one of these attacks off the Puna coast, a fisherman struck Kamehameha on the head with a paddle. The force of the blow was so great it surely would have meant death for any other mortal, but in this instance the paddle broke, not Kamehameha's skull.

When the fisherman was brought to Kamehameha for judgment, he was not punished. Instead, the warrior admitted he had been wrong to lead wanton invasions and instituted Māmalahoe Kānāwai, the Law of the Splintered Paddle, which from then on protected peaceful villagers from senseless attacks by bickering chiefs.

In the pages that follow, more colorful characters from the Big Island's past are introduced. In each chapter, a myth or story related to the district or districts under discussion stands side by side with text about the area. Walk in the footsteps of the people of old, and immerse yourself in the spirit of this extraordinary place. You won't be disappointed. The Big Island promises big surprises and even bigger rewards.

Hilo and Hāmākua

AN ETERNAL EDEN

One afternoon, Pele, the volcano goddess, amused herself by watching her fires smolder in Kīlauea, the gigantic crater that was her home. Her sisters sat nearby, weaving lei of bright red lehua blossoms from the 'ōhi'a (a tree native to Hawai'i). Glancing up, one of the sisters saw a handsome young man standing on a hill, looking at them. "Let's ask him to come and visit us," she said, pointing him out to her sisters. "We can show him our lei and drape some around his neck."

"What are you talking about?" Pele scoffed. "I don't see a man; I only see a pig. That is Kamapua'a, the pig."

Her sisters protested, "How can you say he is a pig? Pigs have snouts, pigs have tails!"

But Pele was adamant. "I recognize you," she shouted to the young

Nurtured by frequent rains, Hilo, the Big Island's county seat, and the northern Hāmākua Coast wear a perpetual cloak of green. Because of the abundant water supply, sugarcane plantations flourished here for more than a century. Bordering the fifty-mile stretch of blacktop that leads from Hilo to Waipi'o Valley are little villages with lyrical names—Honomū, Laupāhoehoe, Honoka'a, Kukuihaele. Also embellishing the landscape are magnificent forests, orchards, gardens, and valleys, the most celebrated of which is Waipi'o. Kamehameha I grew up in this sacred place and

man. "I know who you are—Kamapua'a, the pig with a long snout; Kamapua'a, the pig with a wagging tail!"

Pele's words angered the visitor, who was indeed Kamapua'a, the pig god from O'ahu who could appear as a man or a hog at will. He returned Pele's insults with equal animosity. "And you are red-eyed Pele!" he retorted. "You cause it to rain in the lowlands—not life-sustaining rain, but destructive rain of rocks and hot lava!"

Now the tempers of both demigod and demigoddess were lit. Pele commanded her brothers to ignite the fires in Kīlauea, and molten lava spewed forth, rocks shot up like bullets, and the air became thick with steam and smoke. Dark clouds hid the sun, lightning flashed, and thunder resounded with such force that the earth quaked. Pele was pleased; surely this display of power would drive the impudent pig god back to O'ahu.

But when the fires died and the air cleared, there was Kamapua'a, standing tall and defiant on the same hill. Enraged, Pele ordered her

This stunning view of the Waipi'o Valley shoreline can be seen from the Waimanu Valley Trail.

returned to it often in later years, finding solace in its peace and beauty. Indeed, pristine Waipi'o possesses a healing spirit. Taro, bananas, avocados, coconuts, passion fruit, guavas, lemons, limes, breadfruit, mountain apples, coffee, and grapefruit grow here in glorious disarray. Birdsong harmonizes with the soothing voice of Hi'ilawe, Hawai'i's highest single waterfall, which plunges more than one thousand feet to the valley floor.

Standing guard over it all is a stoic sentinel who wears a helmet of snow in the winter—lofty, regal Mauna Kea, the White Mountain.

brothers to rekindle Kīlauea's fires. This time, Kamapua'a prayed to the gods of the skies, asking rain to fall heavily on the earth.

In response to his prayers, the heavens did weep. Rain poured down in torrents, quenching the flames in Kīlauea. Water filled the crater and flowed over its rim. Still, this was not enough to cool the tempestuous fire goddess; furious, she once again directed her brothers to set Kīlauea ablaze.

Tiring of the battle, Kamapua'a called out to Pele: "It is pointless to fight; let's be friends!"

Her sisters and brothers concurred. "Make peace with him now, Pele, or our home will be left a wasteland."

Pele relented. "Fire and water are equally strong; I cannot destroy him, and he cannot destroy me. Very well, Kamapua'a, we have a truce."

As part of the agreement, the island of Hawai'i was divided between them. Pele still rules over the arid regions of Ka'ū, Puna, and Kona, but the lush northeastern sector is the domain of Kamapua'a.

A graceful strand of glistening silver, Hi'ilawe Falls stands out amid the emerald green of Waipi'o Valley.

*F*ragrant *kāhili* ginger adorns the Hāmākua Ditch Trail in Waipi'o Valley, home to many great chiefs in ancient times, including Kamehameha I.

*H*ilo, America's other "city by the bay," wraps around picturesque Hilo Bay.

*T*he remodeled Koehnen Building in downtown Hilo dates back to 1910.

*S*uisan Fish Market in Hilo is the site of a lively auction that takes place at 7:30 A.M. daily, except Sunday.

A simple pagoda provides the perfect meditation spot in Hilo's lovely Lili'u-okalani Gardens, formal Japanese gardens accented with stone lanterns, half-moon bridges, ponds, and streams.

*T*he centerpiece
of a lush state park,
'Akaka Falls tum-
bles 442 feet into a
foliage-lined pool.

*A*frican tulips
decorate a
Hāmākua Coast
stream with vivid
splashes of color.

FACING PAGE:

*R*elentless surf batters the rocky Laupāhoehoe coastline.

*Y*oung people explore the breakwater at Laupāhoehoe (left). Ironwood trees flourish along the shore in the area (right). In 1946 a tidal wave roared along the Hāmākua Coast near Laupāhoehoe Beach Park, taking the lives of twenty-three schoolchildren and three adults.

𝒜 black sand
beach fringes the
entrance to sacred
Waipi'o Valley,
whose archaeo-
logical treasures
include the vestiges
of two *heiau* (tem-
ples), Paka'alana
and Hanua'aloa.

𝓕requent rains
nurture all kinds
of flora along the
Hāmākua Coast,
among them the
flowering paperbark
tree, a transplant
to Hawai'i from
Australia.

*I*n Waipi'o, *lo'i* (irrigated terraces) for growing taro are tended by a handful of farmers who relish the seclusion the valley offers. When Captain Cook arrived in Hawai'i in 1778, there were four thousand people living in Waipi'o. Today the valley claims only about fifty residents.

*T*he steep road into Waipi'o Valley is traversable only by four-wheel drive.

FACING PAGE:

*H*ere's country living at its best: nature stands guard as children frolic in the cool Waipi'o Stream.

*C*oconuts, leaves, and stones create interesting patterns on Waipi'o Valley's black sand beach.

The native *hāpuʻu* fern blankets much of the landscape along the Hāmākua Coast.

A hiker makes his way through dense ginger growth along the Waipiʻo Valley Ridge Trail.

Waterfalls plummet down the slopes of Waimanu Valley.

FACING PAGE:

*S*now in Hawai'i? As amazing as it may seem, snow blankets the summit of Mauna Kea every winter.

*S*een from Mauna Kea, sunset paints the sky off Waikoloa to the west with broad strokes of vivid color.

*C*louds hover along the western flank of Mauna Kea.

*L*ooking as though they were transported from another planet, thirteen state-of-the-art observatories are strategically positioned on the 13,796-foot summit of Mauna Kea, deemed the best site in the world for astronomical research. The observatories are sponsored by eleven countries, including the United States, France, Japan, Brazil, Taiwan, the Netherlands, and Great Britain. America's twin Keck optical/ infrared telescopes are so powerful they can zero in on a car's headlights from a distance of 15,500 miles.

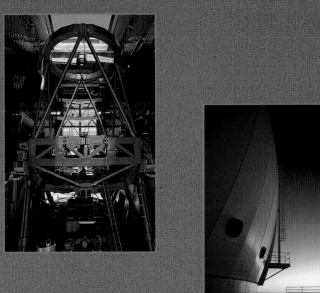

*I*n preparation for their mission to the moon in July 1969, astronauts Neil Armstrong, Buzz Aldrin, and Mike Collins tested their modules on Mauna Kea's barren, lunar-like surface.

North and South Kohala

SIMPLICITY AND SOPHISTICATION

Long ago, Pueo, the owl, and 'Iole, the rat, lived in a fertile area of Kohala. Because sunlight blinded him, Pueo, an industrious farmer, tended his sweet potatoes at night—digging weeds, planting slips, and ensuring his prized patch was well irrigated. Large and lazy 'Iole, meanwhile, preferred to pilfer the plants that Pueo and other farmers had worked long and hard to grow.

One night, the owl noticed some of his plump potatoes had been eaten right off the vine. Evidence of gnawing led him to believe that 'Iole was the culprit. "How dare he steal my food!" Pueo thought. "I'll keep an eye out for him and punish him."

Night after night, Pueo kept careful watch over his garden, but 'Iole was nowhere to be seen. And then it was time to harvest. The owl was counting on a big, healthy crop, and he could hardly wait to taste the fruits of his labor. He pulled the top of one potato and it came out of the earth easily, for there was just the potato top, nothing else! Down the rows of the patch Pueo went, and the result

Paniolo Day festivities showcase the talents of Waimea's keiki *(children).*

Cattle graze contentedly as sunrise casts a golden glow over Parker Ranch pastureland, Waimea.

Those hunting for a breath of fresh air, both literally and figuratively, head for North Kohala, where cane was king during the nineteenth century and most of the twentieth. Today, with the sugar plantations gone, people live in quiet, secluded North Kohala by choice. Here are quaint towns that are little more than a few blocks long, a profusion of fruit trees, exuberant displays of flowers, meadows as wide as lakes, and pristine valleys that seldom are disturbed by human voices or footprints.

Important chapters in Hawai'i's history were written in North Kohala. Kamehameha I was born near fifteen-hundred-year-old Mo'okini Heiau, where his post-birth rituals were held. At Lapakahi State Historical Park, the remnants of rock shelters, house and burial sites, canoe sheds, fishing shrines,

was the same each time. The cunning 'Iole had burrowed under the vines and, unseen, had eaten every potato.

Angered and dejected, Pueo gathered the sweet potato tops, thinking he would at least get a few meals out of them. He filled the imu (underground oven) with heated stones, placed the tops inside, and covered the pit. He went to finish other chores while the vegetables cooked.

When Pueo returned and opened the imu, he found only scraps left inside; while he was away 'Iole had come and stolen most of the food. Pueo could not believe his eyes. Greatly distressed, he ate a few bites and stored the rest in a gourd for a small meal the next day. But when he next checked the gourd, he found it empty; the wily 'Iole had gnawed a hole in the container and eaten the last bits of sweet potato.

Days passed, and Pueo grew weak from hunger. 'Io, the hawk, saw him and asked what was wrong. The owl explained his plight, and his friend promised to help. "I will kill the scoundrel! Let's find him!"

Off they went to 'Iole's home. The rat thought he had been so shrewd that Pueo would not suspect him. He came out to greet his visitors, but before a word came out of his mouth, 'Io pounced on him and tore him into little pieces (the site in North Kohala where 'Iole was killed bears his name). That is the reason rats are small in size today and why they fear the owl and the hawk. That is also why Pueo is no longer a farmer but instead is a zealous hunter of rats.

In 1790 Kamehameha I built Pu'ukoholā Heiau in honor of the war god Kūkā-'ilimoku on the advice of a *kahuna* (priest) who told him he would unify the Hawaiian Islands only after he did so. This war temple has been designated a National Historic Site.

and salt pans provide valuable clues as to what life in a coastal fishing and farming village was like six hundred years ago. Similarly, the Bond Estate—a complex of homes, a school, and a church—turns back the hands of time to the mid-nineteenth century, when devout New England missionaries proselyted throughout the area.

Verdant pastureland carpets Waimea, home of 225,000-acre Parker Ranch, the largest ranch in the state and one of the largest in the country. Waimea is gorgeous on a sunny day—and even more so when the morning mist drifts in and drapes the pastoral setting in the lightest, sheerest of veils.

Kohala's most imposing landmark is Pu'ukoholā Heiau, the last major temple built in Hawai'i. Other archaeological gems—including petroglyph fields, cave shelters, house sites, fishing shrines, ancient footpaths, and fishponds where mullet was raised for the *ali'i* (royalty)—are woven in a necklace of resorts along the sunny coastline of South Kohala. Posh oases in an otherwise desolate lava landscape, these resorts rank among the finest in the world.

FACING PAGE:

*P*ololū Valley's shoreline is a panorama of breathtaking wilderness.

*T*he paved road ends where the scenic Pololū Valley Trail begins. From the lookout at the trailhead, hikers can make it down to the valley floor in about fifteen minutes— the strenuous return journey can take twice as long.

*S*unrise imbues the Big Island's northern coast with a mystical aura. Rugged and remote, this magnificent twelve-mile area stretches between Pololū and Waipi'o valleys.

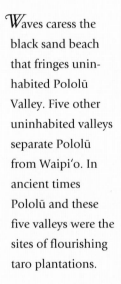

*W*aves caress the black sand beach that fringes uninhabited Pololū Valley. Five other uninhabited valleys separate Pololū from Waipi'o. In ancient times Pololū and these five valleys were the sites of flourishing taro plantations.

A portion of the Kohala Ditch Trail slips behind the long, shimmering veil that is Kapaloa Falls.

*C*actus and other
exotic plants thrive
in North Kohala,
where life and the
landscape have
changed very little
in the past one
hundred years.

*M*ist shrouds
a luxuriant section
of the Kohala
Ditch Trail.

Kamehameha I
is said to have been
born near 1,500-
year-old Moʻokini
Heiau, which was
supposedly built in
a single night by
18,000 men who
formed a human
chain and passed
stones for the tem-
ple hand to hand
from Pololū Valley,
fourteen miles
away. Hawaiians
today still use the
grounds for reli-
gious ceremonies.

*S*et beside the sea, Lapakahi State Historical Park harbors the remnants of a six-hundred-year-old Hawaiian fishing village, now partially reconstructed.

FAR RIGHT:

*L*ong ago, Hono-ipu Landing was a popular spot for surfing. On a clear day you can see Maui in the distance.

*L*ei making, *kapa* (tapa) making, and fashioning ti leaf rain capes are among the demonstrations at Pu'ukoholā Heiau's annual Cultural Festival.

*M*aster masons, the Hawaiians built Pu'ukoholā Heiau with no mortar.

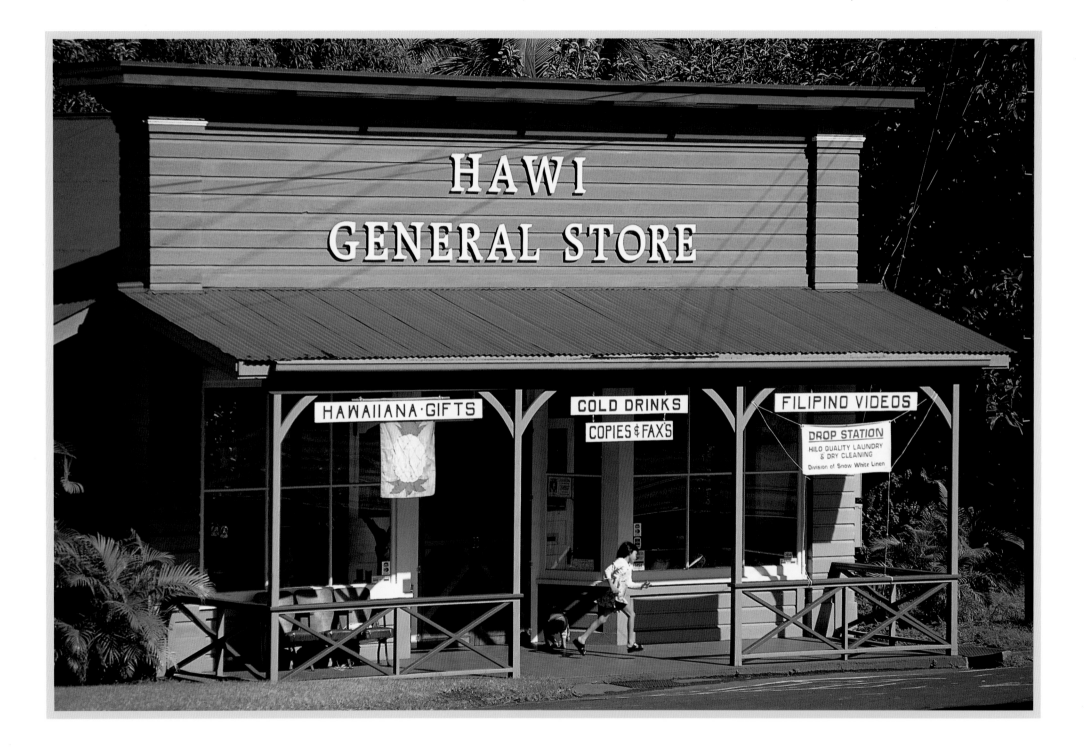

The clock seems to have stopped decades ago in Hāwī, which once was a bustling sugar plantation town. Stroll around town and you'll find wonderful art galleries, clothing boutiques, and restaurants, including Bamboo, which offers a surprisingly sophisticated menu for its rustic setting.

Special events in
Kohala—many of
them centered
around the area's
paniolo (cowboy)
heritage—bring
out a rainbow of
beautiful colors,
costumes, and faces.

*A*t Parker Ranch rodeos, the best cowpokes in the state exhibit their prowess at riding and roping. Lots of thrills and occasional spills are all part of the show.

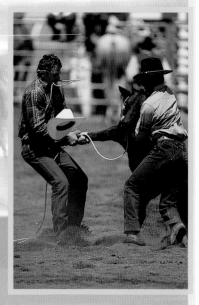

*T*his pastoral Parker Ranch scene could be right out of a Hollywood western.

*W*orkers harvest cabbage in Waimea, where cool temperatures and frequent rains provide ideal growing conditions for a wide variety of crops.

*W*aimea's quaint Keola Mau Loa Church dates back to 1931.

*A*rchaeologists often debate the meanings of the intriguing carvings in lava called petroglyphs. Were they merely doodles of bored passersby? Were they a means of chronicling major historical events? Or did they have religious significance? It makes fascinating food for thought as you roam through easily accessible petroglyph fields in Puakō and ʻAnaehoʻomalu on the Kohala Coast.

65

FAR LEFT:

A lovely crescent of soft white sand, Kauna'oa Beach, which fronts the Mauna Kea Beach Hotel, draws dozens of sun lovers every day.

*T*ake the time to explore Hāpuna Beach State Park and you'll make marvelous discoveries, including this sea cave tucked at its southern end.

*S*waying coconut palms frame a fishpond in 'Anaeho'omalu. In olden times, mullet, *moi*, and other fish were raised in ponds like this solely for the consumption of the *ali'i* (royalty).

*T*he tropical beauty of Kauna'oa Beach and the cluster of otherworldly observatories atop Mauna Kea's bleak summit illustrate two diverse faces of the Big Island.

In ancient times, coconut palms like this one on Kauna'oa Beach provided food and materials used in the making of bowls, utensils, mats, and baskets.

Teamwork, rhythm, strength, and endurance are all essential in the sport of outrigger canoe racing.

FACING PAGE: The playful Pacific refreshes the shores of Kauna'oa Bay with salt-laden spray.

*S*wimming, snorkeling, sailing, boogie boarding— Hāpuna Beach's warm, clear waters are perfect for splashy diversions of all kinds.

Kona

HIDDEN TREASURES

*S*unset embraces Pu'uhonua o Hōnaunau.

*F*ierce *ki'i* (statues) carved from native *'ōhi'a* wood stand guard at Pu'uhonua o Hōnaunau.

Along a quiet stretch of sand at Ka'ūpūlehu, far from the rain-soaked mountains where it normally would be found, a freshwater spring bubbles up from the salty sea. It is an odd phenomenon that supposedly came to be long, long ago, when the land was still young and powerful gods mingled with mortals.

At that time, a chiefess ruled in peace over Ka'ūpūlehu and the neighboring districts of Kūki'o and Manini'ōwali. Then came a terrible drought. Without water, plants could not grow, and the villagers were soon left with nothing to eat. Weakened from hunger, many fell ill. In desperation, the chiefess consulted a kahuna (priest) to find out what needed to be done to bring life back to the land and her people.

The kahuna offered many prayers and returned to the chiefess with this response: "You must fast and remain celibate for ten days to cleanse yourself from past sins. You must also implore your brother, Kāne, the god of living waters, Kāne, the life-giver of our world, to replenish the earth and restore nourishment to your people."

Ka'ūpūlehu (literally "roasted breadfruit") lies near the northern border of the Kona district, which most visitors recognize for its superb fishing and robust coffee. Kona's most valuable asset, however, still goes largely unnoticed; unbeknown to many, it harbors one of the richest troves of archaeological treasures in the Hawaiian archipelago. Within its boundaries can be found the remnants of ancient villages and battlegrounds, grassy slopes for riding *hōlua* (sleds), lava-tube burial caves, fishponds, *pu'uhonua* (places of refuge), petroglyphs, *kū'ula* (stone fishing shrines), and *heiau* (temples).

History maintains a powerful presence in Kona. Kauikeaouli, Kamehameha III, was born near Keauhou Bay, and it was at neighboring Kealakekua Bay that Captain James Cook met his demise. Built of roughly hewn lava stone and mortar made of

The chiefess did as the priest advised, and at the end of her ten-day period of purification, a stranger appeared, whom she immediately recognized as Kāne. The great life-giving god surveyed the grim scene around him and instructed all the men who were able to walk to gather as much firewood as they could and bring it to him.

When they returned with the wood, Kāne told them to dig an imu *(underground oven) and bring it to a high heat. The men were mystified, for there was no food to be cooked, but they did as Kāne asked.*

Kāne then directed them to spread the imu *with many layers of* 'ākulikuli *(a coastal herb) and* makaloa *(a sedge). When this was done, he laid down in the* imu *and ordered the men to keep piling on dirt and* makaloa *until he and the pit were completely covered. The men tried, but no matter how much dirt and* makaloa *they put on, they couldn't cover the* imu; *it kept getting deeper.*

As they were discussing what they could do to solve this dilemma, Kāne suddenly appeared in the sea, and from the place where he stepped forth gushed a freshwater spring. He told the men to uncover the imu, *and when they did, they found steaming heaps of taro, sweet potatoes, breadfruit, yams, and arrowroot. The chiefess and her people ate their fill and expressed their gratitude to their divine patron. Thus ended the devastating famine and drought in Ka'ūpūlehu.*

Robust Kona coffee is grown at more than five hundred farms in the Kona area. Before coffee became the pride of Kona, farmers experimented with many different crops, including sugarcane, tobacco, and sisal.

A sea cave opens to the clear blue expanse of Honomalino Bay.

crushed coral and *kukui* (candlenut tree) oil, Moku-'aikaua Church in Kailua-Kona is the oldest Christian church in Hawai'i. Hulihe'e Palace, overlooking the sea, was a favorite summer retreat of King Kalākaua and other *ali'i* (royalty). And Ahu'ena Heiau, which anchors the northern end of town, is where Kamehameha I meditated and conferred with his advisers and *kāhuna* (priests).

Kona's landscape is defined by rugged expanses of lava as dark as the wings of the 'alalā (Hawaiian crow) and by gardens and orchards that shimmer like emeralds when refreshed by the morning dew. In Kona, the wind rarely speaks louder than a whisper, and the ocean is as clear and blue as the sky. And at the end of each day, the sun relinquishes its reign in silent, stirring splendor.

FAR LEFT:
*D*edicated in 1837, Moku'aikaua Church in Kailua-Kona town is the oldest Christian church in Hawai'i. It was built from rough-hewn lava stone and mortar made from crushed and burned coral mixed with *kukui* nut oil.

*N*estled by the sea, lovely Hulihe'e Palace (marked by its green roof) is another Kailua-Kona landmark.

*T*our boats, yachts, fishing vessels, outrigger canoes dwarfed by mammoth cruise ships—watercraft of all kinds ply the tranquil waters of Kailua Bay.

A bright Christmas bow festoons Hulihe'e Palace's ornate iron gate.

*H*ula is always a highlight of celebrations at Hulihe'e Palace, built in 1838 as the residence for the Big Island's second governor, John Adams Kuakini.

*H*eld during Labor Day weekend in September, the Queen Liliʻuokalani Outrigger Canoe Races cover eighteen miles between Kailua-Kona and Hōnaunau. About 2,500 paddlers participate in this competition, which holds the distinction of being the world's largest long-distance canoe race.

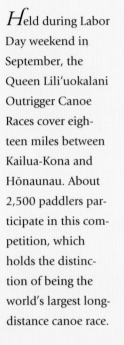

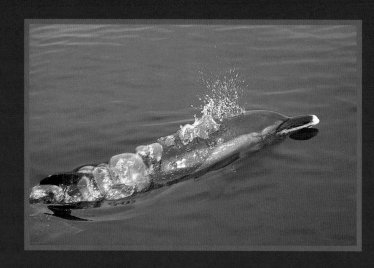

The Kona Coast
is home to an
array of marine life,
including spotted
dolphins, spinner
dolphins, white-
tip sharks, and
pilot whales.

Snorkelers are treated to up-close views of colorful schools of fish, including blue-lined snapper and, if they're lucky, the Hawaiian green sea turtle, which is an endangered species.

*K*ona's Hawaiian International Bill-fish Tournament attracts the world's best anglers. Here, a 587-pound marlin fights for freedom. It lost the battle.

*L*ong ago Pu'uho-nua o Hōnaunau was a sanctuary for defeated warriors and people who had broken the *kapu* (taboos). Today the 180-acre site is a national historical park preserving three *heiau* (temples), models of traditional *hale* (houses), petroglyphs, fishponds, a variety of native Hawaiian plants, and a massive stone wall measuring a thousand feet long, ten feet high, and seventeen feet wide.

FACING PAGE:

*M*en, women, and children representing ancient *ali'i* (royalty) make their way to the beach at Pu'uhonua o Hōnaunau for a traditional purification ceremony.

*V*isitors to the park can enjoy demonstrations of hula, *lau hala* (pandanus leaf) weaving, *kapa* (tapa) making, and traditional Hawaiian games and musical instruments.

Kaʻū and Puna

BEAUTY AMID DESOLATION

Renowned Hawaiiana scholar Mary Kawena Pūkuʻi first learned about her ʻaumakua, her family god, when she was a little girl growing up in Kaʻū. One gloomy day, Kawena got a craving for nenue *(chub fish). There was none in the house, and torrential rains were falling; it obviously was not a good day for fishing. Disappointed, she sat in a corner crying softly because she desired* nenue *so much and could not have it.*

Kawena's auntie noticed the sad child and asked what was wrong. When the girl told her, the auntie said, "Let's go see my uncle."

The two walked to the cave where the old man lived. "Such bad weather!" he exclaimed after he had welcomed them. "Why are you outside today?"

"Kawena longs for nenue *fish," the auntie said.*

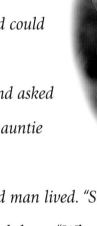

Fringed by frothy waves, Kaʻū is known as a fertile fishing area. From the lonely, windswept coast of Ka Lae, the southernmost point in the United States, anglers launch small boats that carry their lines out where the *ulua* (jack fish) and *ʻahi* (yellowfin tuna) run. Today few dare to venture into the churning sea at Ka Lae, for its strong and merciless currents have swept away even the most experienced of sailors and fishermen. Historians believe Ka Lae may have been the first land sighted by Polynesians migrating from the south around A.D. 750. Deep holes dug into the solid shoreline rock may have served as moorings for these early voyagers' canoes. Legend also designates

"Then she shall have it," the old man declared. With his fishnet in hand, he headed for the beach. Kawena and her auntie followed and watched as he waded into the ocean and cast his net. In a minute he pulled up a mass of wriggling fish. He selected one and threw it back into the bay, saying, "The first one is for you." As if on cue, a shark appeared and snapped up the fish.

"These are for the child," the old man continued, handing four fish to Kawena.

As the shark swam away, the old man said to the little girl, "That is our guardian." And then he began telling a story. "A long time ago, I found my older brother lying still on the sand, as though he were dead. He opened his eyes and saw me standing over him, looking very concerned. In a weak voice, he asked me to bring him 'awa (kava, a narcotic beverage) and bananas.

"As I went to do as he asked, he struggled to his feet and clung to a rock. He scanned the bay as though he were looking for someone and called out, 'Wait, my guardian! The boy is bringing back food.' Then, exhausted, he fell back on the sand. I looked around but didn't see anyone.

"I returned with the 'awa and bananas, and my brother once again made a valiant effort to stand. He called out, 'Come, my guardian!

The Puna Coast Trail begins along the Chain of Craters Road in Hawai'i Volcanoes National Park and hugs the eastern coastline for twelve scenic miles.

Ka Lae as a *leina a ka 'uhane* (literally, "leap of the soul"), a place where the spirits of the dead jumped into the netherworld.

From Ka Lae, the vast district of Ka'ū meanders fifty miles north and almost forty miles from east to west, embracing massive Mauna Loa, which literally means "long mountain"; Kīlauea, home of Pele, the fire goddess; and the great Ka'ū Desert, where warriors who fought against Kamehameha I were supposedly killed by toxic volcanic fumes, mud, and ash showered on them by Pele. Many believe she still roams the region, most often taking the guise of a beautiful maiden, a hobbling old woman, or a little white dog. Such is the magic and mystique of Ka'ū.

The neighboring Puna district reflects the same curious juxtaposition of beauty and bleakness. Over the years, fiery volcanic eruptions have consumed

Come and eat!' I then saw a large shark in the water right below us. My brother fed the shark 'awa and bananas until it was satisfied and thanked it for saving his life. The shark then disappeared in the waves as suddenly as it had appeared.

"Feeling better, my brother told me an incredible story. His canoe had capsized in a squall. The wind and waves carried it away, and he was certain he was going to drown. Then he felt something firm and strong beneath him. He gripped it, thinking at first it was a rock, but it began to move and he realized he was riding on the back of a great shark. The shark carried him to shallow water, and my brother was able to stagger to the beach. That's where I found him.

"From then on my brother often brought his benefactor 'awa and bananas. And sometimes the shark drove fish into the bay for him to eat. Before he died, my brother said I must take care of the creature that saved his life and that it would take care of me. We must always remember our guardian, Kawena."

And until the day she died, Kawena did.

Macadamia nuts mature on a tree in Ka'ū. The Big Island produces 95 percent of the state's macadamias.

Hundreds of lava rocks were used to build this goat corral along the Puna Coast Trail.

ancient *heiau* (places of worship), *ala* (stone-paved trails), the Queen's Bath (a natural freshwater pool where the *ali'i*, or royalty, bathed), and other significant archaeological sites. Yet, interestingly, Puna also is a place of abundance and vitality; ginger root, bananas, papayas, anthuriums, and orchids all flourish in its nutrient-rich volcanic soil.

Cape Kumukahi in Puna is the namesake of a seafarer from Kahiki (Tahiti) who settled here with his two wives. The women are said to have been able to change the seasons as they fancied by nudging the sun back and forth between them. As the easternmost point in the state, Kumukahi, meaning "origin, beginning," is aptly named; each day it is the very first place in the Hawaiian Islands to bask in the light and warmth of dawn.

*B*edecked in beautiful costumes and adornments made of ferns, flowers, shells, and nuts, performers at the Hula Fest in Wai'ōhinu, Ka'ū, share their aloha.

FACING PAGE:

*R*oiling surf meets an unyielding wall of lava at Honu'apo Bay, Ka'ū.

A section of smooth *pāhoehoe* lava provides the perfect "board" for a game of *kōnane* (Hawaiian checkers).

*P*una's rich volcanic soil nourishes a wonderful assortment of plants, among them anthuriums (background and left inset), the *nuku 'i'iwi* or beaked vine (right inset), and ginger root and orchids (facing page).

Volcano

Native to the Himalayas, the *kāhili* ginger, unlike other members of the large ginger family, grows well in cool areas such as Volcano. It gets its name from its resemblance to the *kāhili*, the feather standard that was symbolic of Hawaiian royalty.

Sparks fly and the earth glows; few sights can match the awesome beauty of Pele's pyrotechnics.

Of all the formidable figures in the Hawaiian pantheon, the best known is undoubtedly Pele, the goddess of fire. Like the first inhabitants of Hawai'i, she is said to have come from far-off Kahiki (Tahiti), where, as the story goes, she once got into a heated quarrel with her sister Nāmakaokaha'i, a powerful goddess of the sea. At first it was only a match of words, but then Nāmakaokaha'i commanded huge tidal waves to rush over Pele's lands and home, destroying them.

Realizing she had been defeated, Pele decided to flee Kahiki with other members of her family. Her elder brother, Kamohoali'i, the shark god, provided them with a large sailing canoe and guided them north across the Pacific to Hawai'i. All the while, Nāmakaokaha'i followed them, generating mighty storms in hopes of sinking their canoe.

Searching for a permanent home in Hawai'i, Pele first landed on the island of Kaua'i, where she used her magical spade, Pāoa, to create Pu'u o Pele, the Hill of Pele. For a while, she and her brothers and sisters

The volatile fire goddess Pele definitely has left her mark in the Volcano region, a geologic wonderland of ebony *'a'a* (rough) and *pāhoehoe* (smooth) lava fields, gaping calderas, and searing steam vents that can melt the flesh off a fish in seconds. Also found here, in striking contrast to this starkness, are *kīpuka* (lush pockets of plants and wildlife miraculously spared by raging lava flows) and verdant rain forests where *hāpu'u* ferns and *'ōhi'a* trees grow so densely they block out the sun.

Hawai'i Volcanoes National Park sprawls over 377 square miles, encompassing a visitor center, hotel, restaurant, art center, museum, and observatory where volcanologists keep close tabs on seismic

lived contentedly there, but then Nāmakaokaha'i saw their fires from a high lookout point. She was swift and brutal in her attack, causing water to flow in and extinguish Pele's flames.

Pele then escaped to O'ahu, where she used Pāoa to carve Āliapa'akai (Salt Lake), Pūowaina (Punchbowl), Kohelepelepe (Koko Crater), and Lē'ahi (Diamond Head). From her elevated perch, Nāmakaokaha'i spotted these settlements and once again summoned floods that prevented Pele's fires from burning.

Frustrated, Pele moved on to Moloka'i and then to Maui, but she had no better luck keeping hidden from Nāmakaokaha'i. On the slopes of Haleakalā on Maui, the two sisters engaged in a fierce battle, and it seemed as though Nāmakaokaha'i had killed Pele, leaving huge mounds of broken lava at the base of Haleakalā at a place now known as Nā iwi o Pele (the bones of Pele).

But gazing from her strategic post to the island of Hawai'i, Nāma-kaokaha'i saw the 'uhane, the spirit form, of Pele, floating in red-tinged volcanic smoke. Pele had dug a mammoth pit at Kīlauea and kindled blazing fires within it. Located many miles from the sea, Kīlauea was safely out of Nāmakaokaha'i's reach. With her sister no longer a threat, Pele had found a suitable home at last.

activity. These buildings appear insignificant, however, amid the drama of Nature's beauty; from the tiniest, most delicate of flowers to craters as large as lakes, she reveals her many miracles here. A powerful energy pervades Volcano—a special spirit the Hawaiians call *mana*. As in a church, you enter the area with reverence and awe. You instinctively know that this compelling place must be sacred.

In 1873, British travel writer Isabella Bird was spellbound by the magnificent fury of an eruption in Halema'uma'u Crater: "The prominent object was fire in motion. . . . Before each outburst of agitation there was . . . a throbbing internal roaring. . . . Now it seemed furious, demoniacal, as if no power on earth could bind it, then playful and sportive, then for a second languid, but only because it was accumulating fresh force. . . . It was all confusion, commotion, force, terror, glory, majesty, mystery, and even beauty. And the colour! . . . Molten metal has not that crimson gleam, nor blood that living light!"

*K*ilauea is one of the world's most active volcanoes; over the past 1,100 years, lava from its eruptions has covered nearly five hundred square miles in the Volcano region. Its current eruption began on January 3, 1983—the longest in history—and volcanologists have no idea when it will end.

*D*esolate terrain and the skeletons of dead trees remind hikers of the devastation of past eruptions.

A young girl admires an *'ōhi'a lehua* blossom, the official flower of the island of Hawai'i.

*V*olcano's terrain includes steaming crevices and lush rainforest, as at the entrance to Thurston Lava Tube. Lava tubes form when flowing lava crusts over and the molten core eventually flows away.

*R*ivers of flaming lava hardened into artistic formations when they cooled.

A close look at
the landscape,
plants, and geologic
formations in
Hawai'i Volcanoes
National Park
reveals a montage
of striking textures,
colors, and patterns.

*V*olcano is the heart of the Big Island—a sacred place where gods and goddesses supposedly still dwell and where, in fiery spectacles, new land is born. Wearing the garb and adornments of their ancestors, many Hawaiians come to Volcano to partake of its special spirit and to hold rites that renew their links with the past.

References

Bird, Isabella L. *Six Months in the Sandwich Islands.* Honolulu: University of Hawai'i Press, 1964.

Bisignani, J. D. *Big Island of Hawaii Handbook.* Chico, Calif.: Moon Publications, 1998.

James, Van. *Ancient Sites of Hawai'i: Archaeological Places of Interest on the Big Island.* Honolulu: Mutual Publishing, 1995.

Maguire, Eliza D. *Kona Legends.* Hilo: Petroglyph Press, 1966.

Pūku'i, Mary Kawena. *Hawai'i Island Legends.* Honolulu: Kamehameha Schools Bernice Pauahi Bishop Estate, 1996.

———. *Tales of the Menehune.* Honolulu: Kamehameha Schools Bernice Pauahi Bishop Estate, 1994.

Westervelt, William D. *Hawaiian Legends of Volcanoes.* Rutland, Vt.: Charles E. Tuttle, 1996.

———. *Myths and Legends of Hawai'i.* Honolulu: Mutual Publishing, 1987.

Williams, Julie Stewart. *Kamehameha the Great.* Honolulu: Kamehameha Schools Bernice Pauahi Bishop Estate, 1996.